I AM MORE
BEAUTIFUL THAN...

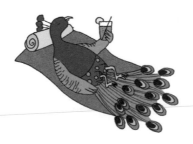

Published and distributed by Knock Knock
1635 Electric Ave.
Venice, CA 90291
knockknockstuff.com
Knock Knock is a registered trademark of Knock Knock LLC
Affirmators! is a registered trademark of Knock Knock LLC

© 2018 Suzi Barrett
Illustrations by Naomi Sloman
Illustrations © 2018 Knock Knock LLC
All rights reserved
Printed in China

ISBN: 978-168349110-1
UPC: 825703-50184-1

10 9 8 7 6 5 4 3 2 1

I AM MORE BEAUTIFUL THAN...

Affirmators!® to Remind You You're More Beautiful Than Just About Anything

Suzi Barrett

KNOCK KNOCK®
VENICE, CALIFORNIA

The key to any positive affirmation is to say it with **conviction**.* The problem is, it's not always easy to feel convincingly confident—especially when life is bullying you with the bad days. For that reason, this book is organized on a scale from 1 to 60, with the easiest to believe Affirmators! in the front of the book, and the much more advanced Affirmators! towards the end.

You can start at the beginning if you need an extra dose of beauty, or just flip around. It's up to you.

*See how we did that?

I am more beautiful than infected gums.

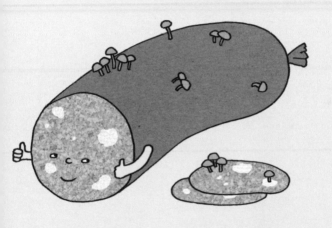

**I am more beautiful
than moldy lunch meat.**

**I am more beautiful
than personal insults.**

I am more beautiful
than tree clip art.

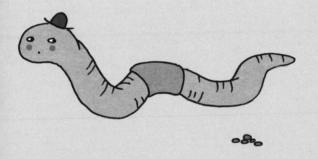

**I am more beautiful
than a worm turdlet.**

October

	1	2	3	4	5	6
7	8	9	10	11	12	13
14	15	16	17	18	19	20
21	22	23	24	25	26	27
28	29	30	31			

I am more beautiful than Medusa's DIY pinup calendar.

I am more beautiful
than algorithmic
screensavers.

I am more beautiful
than the sound of rusty
thumb tacks in a blender.

I am more beautiful
than a first date in a
lighthouse. (But the
lighthouse is haunted.)

I am more beautiful than slow-motion badminton.

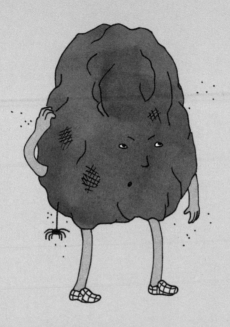

I am more beautiful than that dusty raisin that always turns up under the fridge, even though I never buy or eat raisins.

I am more beautiful than heart-shaped fungus.

I am more beautiful than the sight of an old roommate I feel pretty OK about.

I am more beautiful than anyone's first-grade school photo, take one.

I am more beautiful than bioluminescent chowder.

I am more beautiful than
an ambivalence parade.

**I am more beautiful
than khaki fireworks.**

I am more beautiful than
an unkempt supermodel.

I am more beautiful than
a tattoo of a ladybug.

THE FUTURE SHALL UNFOLD
MAGICALLY AT YOUR FEET

I am more beautiful than
fortune cookie wisdom.

I am more beautiful
than the atrium of the
firefly museum.

I am more beautiful
than giraffe eyelashes.

I am more beautiful
than the smell of old, yet
freshly laundered, socks.

I am more beautiful than a loving twin's birthday text.

I am more beautiful than
newborns dressed as fruit.

I am more beautiful
than the inside of a
wedding cake.

I am more
beautiful than
the sight of the
finish line.

I am more
beautiful than
snowflakes on
a mirror.

**I am more
beautiful than
angel farts.**

I am more
beautiful than
spontaneous
picnics.

I am more
beautiful than
hummingbird
flirtation.

I am more
beautiful than
waterfalls in
zero gravity.

I am more
beautiful than
cloud porn.

I am more beautiful
than harps, played
during a gentle rain.

I am more beautiful
than an all-night
nebula party.

I am more beautiful than
a platypus's first steps.

**I am more
beautiful than
dragon eggs.**

I am more beautiful than a giant, pizza-shaped piñata releasing food onto every starving community on the planet.

I am more
beautiful than
honesty.

I am more beautiful
than a pile of
French bulldogs.

I am more
beautiful than the
northern lights, as
viewed through a
kaleidoscope.

I am more beautiful
than lightning in a
souvenir bottle.

I am more beautiful
than the Italian Riviera,
decorated for an occasion.

I am more beautiful
than an original
Monet...

hologram.

I am more beautiful than
a baby dolphin's love.

I am more beautiful
than Christmas in a
woodland cottage.

I am more beautiful
than Peacock Island.

I am more beautiful
than fairy feasts.

I am more beautiful than first runner-up in a rainbow contest.

I am more beautiful than the sound of an unprompted child expressing gratitude and/or appreciation.

I am more beautiful than an entire ballet performed by the nine Greek muses.

I am more beautiful
than that feeling I had
when everything worked
out even better than I
thought it could.

I am more
beautiful than
Grandma's
belly laugh.

I am more beautiful
than two sunsets,
kissing tenderly.

I am more beautiful
than a chandelier
made of other, much
tinier chandeliers.

I am more beautiful
than music created
by wizard spells.

I am more beautiful than the universe, shot through a cannon, onto a stretched canvas hanging under a black light.

I am more beautiful
than requited love.

**I am more beautiful
than Earth, circa 200 B.C.**

I am more beautiful than turtles doing yoga.